W9-BFG-002

Portage Public Library
2665 Irving Street
Portage, IN 46368

CRESCENT BOOKS

NEW YORK

America's Engineering Marvels

CAROL M. HIGHSMITH AND TED LANDPHAIR

PORTER COUNTY PUBLIC LIBRARY SYSTEM
Portage Public Library
2665 Irving Street
Portage, IN 46368

917.304 HIG   POR
Highsmith, Carol M.
America's engineering
marvels /   JAN 2 7 2004
33410007332788

FOREWORD

A paper clip is an engineering wonder. Consider its timeless design, tensile strength, and versatility. A pencil is a marvel. (How *do* they get the lead in there?) Jet engines, computer circuit boards, orbiting satellites, automobile power steering, microwave ovens, air-conditioning coils, lasers and fiber-optic networks, MRI machines, and synthetic oils are miraculous pieces of work. And let us not forget the mousetrap! These and a thousand other achievements transformed daily life. But we do not regard a zipper or safety pin or electron microscope with the same awe that we behold more imposing structures conceived by the human mind and built by hand by mortal men and women. Never, most likely, have we packed up the family to go see a reaper or a check-out machine that reads bar codes, wonders though they are. This book invites you to great American places that you can visit for yourself, save, tragically, for the World Trade Center towers, which the hand of evil brought down. We stubbornly include them because they deserve a place on the roster of remarkable feats of engineering. No one has yet built a better mousetrap, but what follows are glorious photographs and brief stories of bridges and monuments, highways and skyscrapers and railroad sites (even a roller coaster) that are marvelous in the grandest sense of the word.

The White House, Washington Monument, and Jefferson Memorial are architectural jewels, and the monument is an engineering masterpiece. Weighing 90,854 *tons* (thanks to marble and granite walls ranging in thickness from fifteen feet at the base to eighteen inches on the upper shaft), it rises 555 feet above the National Mall.

WASHINGTON MONUMENT

The Continental Congress had proposed an equestrian statue honoring George Washington, the nation's revered first president. Ten days after Washington died in 1799, the U.S. Congress discussed enshrining his tomb within the new Capitol. In 1801, Washington, D.C., architect Samuel Blodgett distributed a broadside calling for a Washington "Monument or Mausolleum" or "whatever the object of our respect may be called." But nothing got built. Finally in 1833, a citizens' committee raised contributions to sponsor a design contest. The winner, Robert Mills, offered an Egyptian-style obelisk nearly flat on top and surrounded by a Greek colonnade. Work began on the shaft in 1848. The site, on what was then a brambly National Mall, gave promise of a view, from the monument's upper reaches, of Washington's distant Mount Vernon home. Everyone from American Indian tribes to foreign nations donated blocks of marble and granite, many bearing inscriptions. But donations ran out in 1854, and the monument stood like a stump through the Civil War and beyond. In a burst of centennial fervor, Congress appropriated funding in 1876, and construction of the obelisk (streamlined, pointed, and minus the colonnade) resumed. The monument's 3,300-pound marble capstone was set in place on December 6, 1884. Until a construction elevator could be converted for passenger use, visitors climbed 893 steps to the top.

Architect Mills was furious that the monument's Greek colonnade (featuring a heroic Washington figure standing in a chariot among statues of thirty other Revolutionary War heroes) was never built. He likened the final design to "a stalk of asparagus." Others to this day fondly call it "the National Pencil."

CAPITOL DOME

Washington's planner, Pierre L'Enfant, picked Jenkins Hill, the highest spot in town, for his "Congress House," and he envisioned a dome atop the home of the nation's legislature. Architect of the Capitol Charles Bulfinch designed one (a squat, wood affair covered in copper that looked like the base of a plunger). It went up from 1820 to 1822. When Bulfinch's successor, Thomas Walter, began designing wings for the building that would overwhelm the scale of the modest center dome in 1850, members of Congress knew they needed something grander. A year later, fire destroyed most of Congress's library (then housed in the Capitol) and the need for a "fireproof," as well as loftier, dome was assured. Walter took on the challenge and wowed them with his design: a majestic dome with inner and outer cast-iron shells, thirty-six columns, pilasters, and lots of windows, crowned by a heroic statue. Begun in 1855, the job took eight years. President Lincoln insisted that work continue right through the Civil War "as a sign we intend the Union shall go on," and the unfinished rotunda served as Union Army barracks for a time. When construction was complete, almost nine million pounds of iron plates had been bolted together and painted to produce the awe-inspiring 287-foot (fireproof!) dome, rotunda, and porticos that we know today.

After the Capitol's original dome was removed and a temporary roof installed, a steam derrick (powered by wood from the discarded dome) lifted pieces of the new iron dome into place. In addition to the cast-iron walls and marble columns, five million pounds of masonry ring the dome.

Inside the Capitol Dome, Constantino Brumidi's 1865 fresco, *Apotheosis*, is constructed in two rings, the inner representing the Union's thirteen original states, and the outer depicting four hundred years of American history. George Washington's is one of the statues of great Americans in the Capitol Rotunda below.

TRANSCONTINENTAL RAILROAD

It has been likened to man's first walk on the moon one hundred years later. Historian Stephen E. Ambrose called it the end of the Old West and the beginning of the New. When the Central Pacific's wood-burning "Jupiter" engine met the Union Pacific's "No. 119" coal-burner, cowcatcher to cow-catcher, in northern Utah's desolate Promontory Mountains on May 10, 1869, handshakes and toasts were exchanged, and bells pealed across America as a telegrapher sent word that the great transcontinental railroad had linked the vast nation. Four ceremonial spikes, including two of pure gold and one of silver, were driven to mark the occasion. Track-laying crews had toiled relentlessly across the "Great American Desert," Rocky Mountains, and High Sierras. In a single day, a C.P. crew of Irishmen laid ten miles, fifty-six feet worth of 560-pound rails by hand—a record that even machines would never match. The Central Pacific, which had to ship every locomotive, rail, and spike fifteen thousand miles around Cape Horn to Sacramento, had other miracle workers, too: more than ten thousand inde-fatigable Chinese. The transcontinental railroad tied western farms and ranches to markets and cut travel time from weeks by sea or wagon to six or seven days. By finally connecting distant California to eastern states, it truly united the United States.

The original engines at the "wedding of the rails" that bridged the American frontier were scrapped in the early twentieth century, but each day during the temperate months, faithful replicas come together at the Golden Spike National Historic Site, northwest of Brigham City, Utah.

Milepost Zero of
the Union Pacific's
transcontinental line
is marked by a
painted-concrete
Golden Spike
Monument (right) in a
quiet park in Council
Bluffs, Iowa. Only a
fragment of the U.P.'s
original roadbed
west out of Omaha,
Nebraska, across the
Missouri River,
remains (opposite).

Exhibits at the California State Railroad Museum in Sacramento mark the site where the Central Pacific began its push east. One (opposite) depicts Chinese "coolies," as they were disparagingly called, who undertook back-breaking, treacherous tasks along sheer cliffs of the Sierra Nevada Mountains. Hundreds died in avalanches and blasts of volatile black powder. The C.P. passenger terminal's telegrapher's office (above) is also recreated.

BROOKLYN BRIDGE

There was a lot to marvel at when John
Augustus Roebling's magnificent Brooklyn
Bridge was completed across New York's
East River in 1883 after fourteen years of
relentless effort. Roebling had invented
steel wire cable and used it to great effect
on this, the world's first steel cable suspension bridge, which measured an astounding
1.14 miles end-to-end. Roebling's bridge
carried not just horse-drawn wagons but
also trolleys, and he included a magnificent
promenade above the traffic, right down the
middle of the bridge. The vaults of the
bridge's spectacular double-arched towers
have been compared to Roman catacombs,
and the New York-side tower's archways
have been used for everything from
farmers' markets to "Art in the Anchorage"
shows. Roebling's son, Colonel Washington
Roebling, directed the deployment of
airtight iron and wood caissons that were
sunk into the river. Inside several chambers
into which compressed air was pumped,
workers using calcium lamps and sperm
candles dug out the river bottom and laid
limestone blocks for the giant towers.
Not enough was known then about caisson
disease, or "the bends," in which those
who surface from the deep too quickly
suffer excruciating pain, dizziness, and
paralysis. Colonel Roebling himself
contracted the disease after repeated
descents into the caissons, and he withdrew
to spend his last years near the company's
Trenton, New Jersey, wire factory.

Brooklyn was a fiercely independent city
when the Roeblings' bridge went up, and its
citizens, more than Manhattanites, utilized
the beautiful structure. Brooklyn owned and
paid for two-thirds of the bridge (New York
the rest) so the Brooklyn part of the "New
York and Brooklyn Bridge" name endured.

The Brooklyn Bridge's towers were built first. The independent cities of New York and Brooklyn were symbolically linked one August day in 1876 as the bridge's first support cable, affixed to the Brooklyn shoreline anchorage, was lugged across the East River by scow and hauled up the New York tower. Six thousand bystanders cheered as the bridge's master mechanic, Frank Farrington, then *rode* across a second cable in a flimsy boatswain's chair.

Masonry walls alone might hold up cloud-busting buildings if they could be ever-thickened over a massive, pyramidal base swallowing dozens of blocks. But straight upward is the only option in crowded cities. The solution came with the Bessemer process that packed incredible tensile strength into long steel beams that could be riveted into soaring vertical columns—then connected crosswise by girders that allow each floor to support much of its own weight. Sturdy steel cores, minimizing sway in the face of howling winds, evolved as well. Chicago got the jump on skyscrapers with William Le Baron Jenney's ten-story Home Insurance Company Building in 1885. It demonstrated that a steel skeleton could hold up a tall building. But it was New York City's twentieth-century skyscraper parade in classic skyline silhouettes that dazzled the world's imagination. New York had already introduced the first passenger elevator in 1857, sparking daydreams about super-elevated buildings. Imposing symbols of the Machine Age, New York skyscrapers—first of ornamented Art Deco design and later coldly functional in the boxlike International Style—set trends for sky-scrapers everywhere. As Walter Chrysler exclaimed in a brochure for his stylish head-quarters building, skyscrapers symbolize not just technological achievement but also everyman's rise to the top in business.

The triangular, twenty-two-story Flatiron Building (right), erected in 1902, is New York's oldest skyscraper. Desperately wanting his company's Deco headquarters building (opposite) to be the world's tallest in 1930, Walter Chrysler had architect William Van Alen hide the topmost finial until a rival building opened. But Chrysler quickly lost the title to the Empire State Building.

Absent the World Trade Center, the eighty-five-story Empire State Building again dominates Manhattan's skyline. Supported by fifty-seven-thousand tons of structural steel, the utilitarian skyscraper, which opened in April 1931, maximizes office space. Its seventy-three elevators can zip passengers to the eightieth floor in forty-five seconds.

MOUNT RUSHMORE

In the early 1920s Doane Robinson, South Dakota's state historian, dreamed of a panoply of western heroes carved in spires called the "Needles" in the rugged Black Hills. He sounded out sculptor Lorado Taft, known for his classic fountains, but Taft declined. So Robinson turned to Gutzon Borglum, whose work on stone figures of Confederate heroes on Stone Mountain, Georgia, was stalled by a personality conflict. Borglum agreed to search out a Black Hills site that could showcase a monumental work, not about Buffalo Bill Cody and Lewis & Clark but about "America's founders and builders." Beginning in 1927, Borglum and his crews shaped the granite faces of George Washington, Thomas Jefferson, Abraham Lincoln, and Theodore Roosevelt using the sculptor's tricky "pointing" technique, in which carefully placed dynamite charges "carved" more than 90 percent of the work. Workers hanging in boatswain's chairs finished the job with pneumatic drills. "Pointing" involved a calculation, using a giant protractor and a plumb bob, of one inch on the model in Borglum's studio to one foot on the mountain. The sixty-foot faces, five-hundred feet above the new national park's visitor center, were completed and dedicated one at a time, beginning with Washington in 1930 and ending with Roosevelt in 1939. Public contributions paid the remarkably small cost of about $1 million.

Gutzon Borglum found the granite façade of Mount Rushmore perfect for his task. It was sufficiently firm and stable (geologists estimate it will erode an inch every ten thousand years) and offered a southeastern exposure, meaning it would enjoy sunlight much of the day.

RIVERBOAT NENANA

The centerpiece of Pioneer Park in Fairbanks, Alaska, the sternwheel riverboat
S.S. *Nenana* is the world's second-largest
wooden vessel (the first is a San Francisco
sidewheeler ferry, the *Eureka*). The *Nenana*
was built in 1932–33 in Nenana, Alaska, along
the Tanana River, by the Alaska Railroad with
parts shipped from Seattle. Through the late
fifties, in eight round-trips during Alaska's
fleeting ice-free season, the boat hauled
up to 260 tons of freight, thirty-five passengers—and fifteen cords of wood for the
boiler—at five mph upstream and sixteen
mph downstream to villages and gold mines
along the Tanana and Yukon Rivers. Guided
by a mammoth spotlight, the *Nenana* often
churned twenty-four hours a day. Her crew
of thirty-two included cooks, bakers, and
uniformed stewards who served passengers
in style on the boat's long, mahogany
"saloon deck." A favorite menu item: moose.
Forlornly retired, the *Nenana* was floated to
Fairbanks for Alaska's 1967 centennial cele-
bration and turned into a largely ignored
museum and floating hotel. But in 1987,
with support that included a brownie drive
by schoolchildren, restaurant owner Jack
Williams organized the Fairbanks Historical
Preservation Foundation. It began an "inch-
by-inch" restoration that continues. An
onboard diorama, including old photographs
of the *Nenana* in action and scenes along the
river, gives visitors a visual timeline.

The *Nenana*'s winch system included spars called
"walking legs" that swung outward and could
literally "walk" the boat off a sandbar when—as
frequently happened—she got stuck at low tide.
To recapture the boat's historic fabric, restorers
had to remove twenty-two layers of paint.

HOOVER DAM

The rambunctious Colorado River had long
been eyed as an ideal source of water for the
arid Southwest and energy for much of the
West. But it took Bureau of Reclamation
engineers and five thousand men, housed at
an instant "company town" called Boulder
City at the height of the Great Depression,
to tame the tempestuous river by creating
the 6,600,000-ton, sixty-story-high Hoover
Dam across the Black Canyon of the
Colorado on the Nevada-Arizona border,
thirty miles southeast of Las Vegas. First,
the river's water was diverted into tunnels
bored through canyon walls. Then, beginning on June 6, 1933, workers poured
approximately one-hundred-sixty thousand
cubic yards of concrete a month over two
years into forms constructed across the
canyon. Vertical columns were locked
together by a series of blocks ("think giant
Lego set," the dam's website advises) made
of carefully cooled concrete. Grout was then
forced into crevices to complete the structure. The reservoir behind Hoover Dam
captured enough water to cover the state of
Pennsylvania one-foot deep. For fourteen
years, the dam's seventeen generators held
the record as the world's largest hydroelec-
tric power plant. More massive than the
largest of Egypt's pyramids, Hoover Dam
subdued the Colorado, created a sublime
recreation area, and sent water flowing pre-
dictably into California's rich Imperial Valley.

Hoover Dam was named for Herbert Hoover,
incumbent president at the time of its authoriza-
tion in 1928. But the next administration's
Interior secretary, "New Dealer" Harold Ickes,
loathed Hoover, and for years official documents
referred to "Boulder Dam." Congress reaffirmed
the dam's "Hoover" designation in 1947.

GOLDEN GATE BRIDGE

The great "international orange" bridge that opened across the Golden Gate strait in 1937 has become an enduring symbol of the City by the Bay. To understand its engineering, picture an incredibly sturdy hammock, suspended between two massive support towers. Three-foot-thick cables—each a bundle of more than twenty-seven-thousand wires—drape over the bridge's towers, then stretch to bedrock in San Francisco and Marin County. Each cable began with a single wire across which a spinning shuttle wheel rode back and forth, twisting together thousands more wires. The finished cables hold up the "hammock"—the bridge's rigid road surface and railings—suspended below. During four years of construction, eleven men lost their lives in the swirling winds and fast-moving currents. Nineteen others who fell were saved by a safety net and informally inducted into the "Halfway to Hell Club." More notoriously, the Golden Gate Bridge has been the site of almost one thousand suicides. The heaviest load the bridge ever carried was the weight of an estimated three hundred thousand people who marked its fiftieth anniversary by walking across it on May 24, 1987. As of mid-2000, the count of vehicles that had crossed the bridge had topped 1.6 billion. Contrary to urban legend, the bridge is not constantly being painted. Painting corroded components is a touch-up maintenance job.

Explorer John C. Frémont named the strait into San Francisco Bay *Chrysopylae*, or Golden Gate, because it reminded him of Istanbul's Golden Horn Harbor. Until New York's Verrazano-Narrows Bridge opened in 1964, the Golden Gate Bridge, at 1.7 miles, was the world's longest span.

The Golden Gate Bridge has been modified several times, first in the 1950s after a windstorm caused the bridge to undulate. This raised fears of another "Galloping Gertie," the Tacoma Narrows Bridge in Washington state that began oscillating and tore itself in two in 1940. Most recently, the Golden Gate Bridge Authority has retrofitted the bridge to strengthen its resistance to earthquakes.

INTERSTATE HIGHWAY SYSTEM

Arguably the greatest engineering public-works project of the twentieth century was launched in 1956, when construction began on President Dwight D. Eisenhower's dream of a coast-to-coast, border-to-border, high-speed highway system. A military man, he had observed the U.S. Army's first, agonizingly tedious, sixty-two-day transcontinental motor convoy in 1919. Eisenhower had seen Germany's autobahns, and he knew the value of modern highways to homeland defense. An earlier president, Franklin D. Roosevelt, had also extolled the value of limited-access, divided, "inter-regional" highways like the Pennsylvania Turnpike, which had opened in 1940, and he bemoaned the welter of state highway regulations and road standards. Ultimately the federal government agreed to fund 90 percent of the cost of the original, forty-one-thousand-mile, $50-billion Interstate Highway system, which would include mostly free high-speed superhighways and loops and spurs bypassing major cities. By 1975, the interstate system, which represented only 1 percent of the nation's road mileage, carried more than 20 percent of its traffic. One achievement that would have pleased President Eisenhower was the completion of the last few miles of I-5 in central California, after which vehicles could motor between the Mexican and Canadian borders without encountering a single traffic light. In 1994, the American Society of Civil Engineers designated the interstate highway system one of the "Seven Wonders of the United States."

Construction of new cloverleafs and "spaghetti bowls" where interstate highways and city belt-ways connect (as in this juncture of I-15 and I-515 in Las Vegas) continues, seemingly unabated, across the land. Yet another short superhighway, I-215, crosses both I-15 and I-515 a few miles away.

In 1993, Dwight D. Eisenhower's son John and other dignitaries unveiled the new emblem of the interstate highway system (above), which had been renamed for the late president three years earlier. Free-and-easy travel on the system can still be a joy and a treat for the eye in remote stretches like this section of I-70 (right) west of Grand Junction, Colorado.

The term "high-speed" can be a misnomer when interstate highways get close to congested cities like Chicago. Come rush hour, even the widest of interstates can become a (barely) "moving parking lot." Note another of our engineering marvels, Sears Tower, to the far right of the intersection of the John F. Kennedy, Eisenhower, and Dan Ryan Expressways.

BIG BRUTUS

You don't think of Kansas as coal country, but the state once supported thriving strip-mining operations. In 1962 the Pittsburg and Midway Coal Company commissioned a gargantuan, $6.5-million shovel that was crafted in Milwaukee in pieces—some of them weighing 120 tons—shipped to Kansas, and assembled over eleven months. It immediately became the world's second-largest electric shovel; the largest was another Bucyrus-Erie model in southeast Kentucky. A Pittsburg and Midway superintendent, Emil Sandeen, gaped at the sixteen-story-tall, orange behemoth when it was completed and dubbed it "Brutus." It took only a few more glances before the "Big" was added. For eleven years, just three workers at a time maneuvered Brutus, laying bare one square mile of "overburden" a year to expose a nine-million-ton seam of coal. Brutus was an electricity hog; its electric bill approached $27,000 a month. Akin to the stories once heard about prison electric chairs, it's said the lights dimmed in West Mineral, two miles away, whenever operators revved Brutus's two powerful motors. Relocating the metal beast was deemed impractical once its patch of southeast Kansas had been gouged. After it sat, rusting, for a decade, the mining company donated the shovel to Big Brutus, Inc., a regional nonprofit preservation organization that has maintained the monster as a tourist attraction.

Twenty-four hours a day in three shifts, 5,500-ton Big Brutus crept at two-tenths of a mile per hour, scooping out 135 tons of earth with each bite. An operator maneuvered the bucket, a "groundsman" guided Brutus's tanklike treads, and an "oiler" kept up maintenance.

ASTRODOME

Texas has had its share of larger-than-life figures, from Sam Houston and Judge Roy Bean to Lyndon Johnson. And down around the Gulf of Mexico, you'd be well advised to include the son of a bread truck driver, Roy Hofheinz. Once Houston's mayor and a Harris County judge, Hofheinz—as head of the Houston Sports Commission—in 1964 built nothing less than the "Eighth Wonder of the Modern World": the $35-million Astrodome. Circular, 710 feet in diameter, framed by a steel "lamella truss" skeleton with a 9.5-acre footprint, and offering sixty thousand fans unobstructed views, it was the world's first monumental, domed sports stadium. Particularly on notoriously torpid and rainy South Texas summer nights, fans flocked there for the air conditioning and "exploding scoreboard" as much as to watch athletes. Hofheinz set a trend when he ordered luxury "skyboxes" installed for V.I.P. and corporate customers. There was one early problem: Although the Astrodome roof consisted of 4,007 skylights, its prism-effect blinded outfielders and punt catchers. So the glass was painted, but the field's natural grass died. So Hofheinz consulted the Monsanto Corp., which had installed a monofilament synthetic turf called "Chem-grass" on a school field in Rhode Island. Into the cavernous Astrodome went the green-dyed product, soon to be known the world over as "Astroturf."

One Astrodome baseball game, on June 15, 1976, was "rained out" when floodwaters gushed through doorways, inundating the playing field. Although this landmark was supplanted by a downtown stadium with a retractable roof in 2000, the Astrodome still hosts concerts and the world's premier rodeo.

45

ST. LOUIS ARCH

One does not often think of the gleaming arch that anchors the National Expansion Memorial complex on the St. Louis riverfront as tall. Yet the Gateway Arch, which opened in 1967, is the nation's tallest monument. At 630 feet, it's seventy-five feet taller than the Washington Monument. Designed by architect Eero Saarinen, the arch in cross-section is a series of equilateral triangles laid upon one another. Its sections measure fifty-four feet to a side at ground level, tapering to seventeen feet at the top. "Creeper cranes" climbing the arch lifted the double-walled steel sections into place for welding. No scaffolding was used. The sections range in height from twelve feet at the bottom to eight feet in two "keystone" sections where the "legs" of the arch meet. Exterior polished-steel panels are fourteen inches thick. The hollow core is forty-feet-wide at the base but tapers to a snug sixteen feet at the apex. The thirty-two windows (sixteen apiece facing Illinois to the east and Missouri to the west) had to be small to withstand the five-hundred tons of pressure used to pry the legs of the arch apart to insert the last four-foot keystone piece. The Arch is hit by lightning hundreds of times a year, but lightning rods atop the structure detour the current down to bedrock.

Visitors sway up to the Gateway Arch's observation platform inside a tram of eight aluminum capsules that look like cement-mixer barrels. The capsules rotate 155 degrees within a frame on the journey. The weight of the five passengers in each car keeps the capsules upright.

FLATHEAD TUNNEL

Building a dam and reservoir on the
Kootenai River in northwest Montana as
part of a comprehensive plan for the
Columbia River basin was good news for
boaters, cabin owners in the floodplain, and
electric companies looking for new power
sources. But the Libby Reservoir would
submerge the Burlington Northern
Railroad's main line. So in the late 1960s,
with the help of the U.S. Army Corps of
Engineers, the railroad rerouted the line
around the reservoir and straight through
massive Elk Mountain, not far from Glacier
National Park in the Montana Rockies'
Flathead Range. Contractors who worked
on the Flathead Tunnel (the hemisphere's
second-longest railroad tunnel behind the
Cascade Tunnel in Washington state) took
advantage of several technological break-
throughs. For the first time, computers sim-
ulated the operation of trains over the line.
Lasers guided the drilling path with such
accuracy that (even though the tunnel drops
eighty-eight feet along its seven-mile, ten-
foot length) tunneling came within six
inches of meeting perfectly when the
"Rebel" crew advancing from the south met
the "Yankee" team proceeding from
the north. Each operated from four-story,
rail-mounted "jumbo" platforms housing
seventeen drills. On June 21, 1968, President Lyndon Johnson pressed a button in
the White House that set off the final
dynamite charge, completing the "holing
out" process through Elk Mountain.

One needs a good U.S. Forest Service map of
logging roads to find the south portal of what is
now the Burlington Northern–Santa Fe Railroad's
Flathead Tunnel. Its powerful ventilation system
can keep a ten-engine freight from overheating
and flush away diesel fumes after trains pass.

FLATHEAD
TUNNEL
1970

We remember the soaring Twin Towers, 110 stories high, poking through clouds one day, offering crystalline views of places as far away as Greenwich, Connecticut, another. But what also awed visitors was the World Trade Center's sheer mass. Its seven buildings and plaza filled the footprint of 164 previous structures, including two fifty-story buildings. The entire volume of the beloved Empire State Building, it was said, would fit in its *subterranean levels* alone. Fifty-thousand people, from corporate presidents to shoeshine artists, toiled there. Inside the towers' central core, a vertical subway of 239 elevators glided to "local" floors or zipped nonstop to "sky lobbies" on the forty-fourth and seventy-eighth floors. The buildings' skeletal steel beams, coated with anodized aluminum, were set so close together, the towers appeared phosphorescent and windowless from afar. But there were windows aplenty: forty-three thousand of them. The towers were engineered to absorb the impact of a Boeing 707 jet. They did not topple, and their upper floors did not break off, when the ultimate test came one September morning in 2001. But no creation of man could withstand sustained one-thousand-degree fire stoked by jet fuel, and the towers collapsed. With thousands of lives lost, this was a brutal and tragic end for the "monument to world peace" that the Trade Center's designer Minoru Yamasaki said he had in mind.

With the Hudson River nearby, the World Trade Center's contractors faced a groundwater challenge. They ended up setting the buildings inside what were, in effect, concrete "bathtubs" to keep the river at bay. Excavated material helped create entirely new (and free) real estate that became the Battery Park City neighborhood.

The Twin Towers
were 209-foot
squares extended
upward 1,350 feet in
sheer, uninterrupted
lines. Each of the 110
floors offered about
an acre of space.
Closely-spaced steel
columns around the
perimeter created
a "hollow tube"
that supported the
floors and aluminum
"skin." But most of
the vertical support
for each tower was
provided by the
heavy steel columns
surrounding its
elevator core alone.
The towers' working
environment was
described as ethereal
and serene.

SEARS TOWER

Chicago's Sears Tower still loves to play nip and tuck with the Petronas Towers in Kuala Lumpur, Malaysia, for the title of the world's tallest building. Arguments come down to the highest occupied floor, the height of TV antennas, and the measurement at rooftop level. But the Sears Building is a clear winner as the world's largest private office complex. More than sixteen-thousand people work in 101 acres of floor space in the building, which rises one-quarter mile off the ground. Filling two city blocks, the $150-million tower, completed in 1974, is a series of "bundled" square tubes of welded steel, each seventy-five-feet square, and clad in black anodized aluminum and bronze-tinted glass. Nine tubes rise to the fiftieth floor, so in effect, nine separate skyscrapers are combined to form one building. In what's called "stepback geometry," other tubes then terminate at higher floors, creating a staggered silhouette. The separate tubes help protect the building from gale-force blows in this Windy City; still, the building can sway as much as ten inches at the top. So impressive is the Sears Tower that, in the late 1990s, an adjacent street was renamed for its structural engineer, Fazlur Kahn. Sears, Roebuck and Company, which built Sears Tower, has since relocated to a suburban location.

Skidmore, Owings, and Merrill's Sears Tower envelopes more than forty-three-thousand miles of telephone cable, two-thousand miles of electric wire, twenty-five-thousand miles of plumbing, 2,232 steps, and enough concrete to build a five-mile-long, eight-lane highway. It weighs an estimated 222,500 tons.

"Columbia"

SPACE SHUTTLE

Every transportation system has its milk runs. America's space shuttles, history's first reusable spacecraft, carried satellites, the Hubble telescope, and secret military payloads into space; sent work crews to build the international space station; and gave scientific experiments a round-trip ride. Putting together this earth-to-orbit ferry involved unimaginable rocketry, guidance, and thermal technology and the dedication and courage of shuttle crews. Announcing the program in 1972, President Nixon said it would turn the space frontier into "familiar territory" by "routinizing" space travel. Shuttle prototypes—delta-winged for earth re-entry and landing—were tested on piggyback flights atop a 747 jet. On April 12, 1981—twenty years to the day after Soviet cosmonaut Yuri Gagarin blasted off on the world's first spaceflight—a new era in space began with the launch of the *Columbia* orbiter on a two-day mission. It and four subsequent orbiters—named for historic sailing ships—were each a high-tech mélange of two-hundred-thousand synchro-nized components. Muting the accomplish-ment of more than one hundred successes, the *Challenger* explosion in 1986 and the break-up of *Columbia* in 2003, with the tragic loss of fourteen space voyagers between them, cast palls over the program. Never again would shuttle flights be "rou-tinized," but the catastrophes did not douse the nation's determination to continue pushing the boundaries of space exploration.

Mock-ups of a space shuttle orbiter are used to train crews at NASA's Lyndon B. Johnson Space Center outside Houston. Astronauts simulate everything from payload management to house-keeping in space. The complex also includes NASA's Mission Control and the tourist-oriented showcase called Space Center Houston.

SUNSHINE SKYWAY

A badly needed, 4.14-mile bridge across busy Tampa Bay, connecting fast-growing St. Petersburg to faster-growing Bradenton, Florida, proved that solid engineering can be stunning public art. When the Sunshine Skyway opened in 1987, *St. Petersburg Times* editor Andrew Barnes raved that this "wonderful triumph of function and beauty will bring tourists out of their way just to see it." Figg Engineering Group of Tallahassee, Florida, designed the skyway with hurricanes, salinity, and sea traffic in mind. Wind slips past the bridge's twin elliptical piers. Salt in the water and air does not faze its inert, high-performance concrete or the epoxy-coated steel reinforcing bars buried inside. With the main span, which is twelve-hundred-feet long, a full 175 feet above the water, the largest of vessels have "head room" to spare. What turns the $220-million skyway into a tourist attraction are its stays, or soaring steel cables (the longest of which weigh thirty-seven tons) wrapped inside pipes covered in primer, epoxy, and yellow-gold polyurethane paint. Bent through the bridge's 431-foot pylons, the cables give the skyway the look of, as *USA Today* put it, "the rigging of a Space-Age clipper ship." Within twelve years, the Sunshine Skyway won fifteen top engineering and design honors, including a "Night Beautiful" award and the National Endowment for the Arts' Presidential Award.

Unlike the sagging cables of a suspension bridge, the Sunshine Skyway's cable stays (which give the bridge its beautiful twin-sail look) rigidly attach the roadway to 431-foot-high concrete pylons. The longest stay stretches 1,260 feet and contains eighty-two steel strands wrapped inside its yellow-gold-colored cover.

HANGING LAKE VIADUCT

The last piece of Interstate 70 was a remarkable $34-million, double-decker roadway
through Glenwood Canyon in the Colorado
Rockies. Because standard cut-and-fill
blasting would have scarred the breathtak-
ing canyon and dumped rubble into the
rushing Colorado River, state officials
demanded an unobtrusive, environmentally
compatible "stealth bridge" that could
somehow carry four lanes of high-speed
traffic where tired, two-lane U.S. 6 mean-
dered. Figg Engineering Group designed a
snaking two-level viaduct, named for the
picturesque lake that rests on a shelf high
above the canyon. Eastbound lanes were
built mostly at ground level. The challenge
came eighty feet above. There, mostly
hugging the sheer canyon wall, seven
thousand feet of bridgework were assem-
bled in "balanced cantilever" style. Working
symmetrically outward from piers, precast
concrete segments were pieced together
and held taut by bundles of steel tendons
tightened to 891,000 pounds of force. Each
two- to three-hundred-foot segment
consists of the bridge deck atop a hollow,
trapezoidal "box" (ten- to twelve-feet deep),
that diffuses the weight of the roadway and
its traffic downward to the support pier.
Thanks to traveling cranes that crawled on
gantries along the upper deck as the heavy
work proceeded, traffic kept moving down
below. When the viaduct was finished in
1992, the tourist guide to Glenwood Springs
called it "the crowning jewel of the Interstate Highway System."

Flowing like a ribbon, Hanging Lake Viaduct
follows the undulating contours of Glenwood
Canyon and mirrors the geology's horizontal
lines. Horizontal striations on the highway's piers
add to the effect. The long bridge's concrete was
even tinted to blend with the canyon colors.

ROLLER COASTER

If they had the stomach and expense account for it, roller coaster fanatics could ride more than fourteen hundred roller coasters worldwide (over and over again). Russians invented the first coasters about four hundred years ago. They were sleds, flying over snow-covered tracks braced by wooden scaffolding. In 1884, La Marcus Thompson, "the father of the gravity ride," opened a six-hundred-foot, slow-moving "Switchback Railway" at Brooklyn's Coney Island. Faster, clackety wooden roller coasters that followed worked on gravity alone: A chain mechanism ratchets the cars to the top of the first hill and (cue the screams!) releases them. They then traverse the gut-wrenching course unaided until a series of brakes slows the cars into a station. Among aficionados, "air time," or "hang time," is a roller coaster's biggest rush. As one coaster maniac, riding "The Raven" at Holiday World in Santa Claus, Indiana, explained it, "You're going over a hill, and you still have vertical g's pulling you up. The cars yank you down, and it lifts you out of your seat and gives you that 'belly feeling.'" Modern, somersaulting steel coasters use a variety of motors and magnets to thrill (or terrorize) riders at breakneck speeds over parabolic hills and into hairpin turns. On some of the most diabolical "scream machines," riders stand, tightly harnessed, through the ordeal.

As of January 2003, "The Beast" (opposite) at Paramount's Kings Island, near Cincinnati, Ohio, was the world's longest wooden roller coaster, at seventy-four hundred feet. The park's "Son of Beast" (left) was the tallest (twenty-one stories), fastest (seventy-eight mph), and only looping wooden roller coaster on earth.

Photographs copyright © 2003 by Carol M. Highsmith
Text copyright © 2003 by Random House Value Publishing,
a division of Random House, Inc., New York

All rights reserved under International
and Pan-American Copyright Conventions.

No part of this book may be reproduced or transmitted in any form or by any means
electronic or mechanical including photocopying, recording, or by any information
storage and retrieval system, without permission in writing from the publisher.

This 2003 edition published by Crescent Books, an imprint
of Random House Publishing, a division of Random House, Inc., New York.

Crescent is a registered trademark and the colophon is a trademark
of Random House, Inc.

Random House
New York • Toronto • London • Sydney • Auckland
www.randomhouse.com

Printed and bound in Singapore

A catalog record for this title is available from the Library of Congress

ISBN: 0-517-21953-0

9 8 7 6 5 4 3 2 1

Project Editor: Ronald R. Palmer

Designed by Robert L. Wiser, Silver Spring, Maryland

All photographs by Carol M. Highsmith

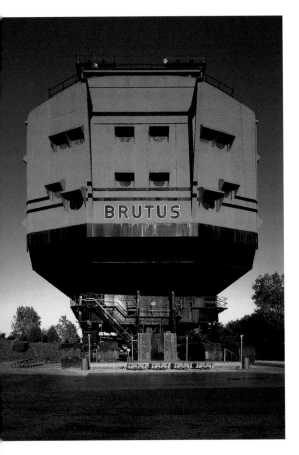

Rotating 360 degrees on a turret, "Big Brutus,"
a humongous electric strip-mining coal shovel
that dwarfs its visitors, could lift a 135-ton
load 101 feet in the air and dump it 150 feet
away. See pages 42–43 for Brutus's story.

Majestic Mount Rushmore in South Dakota's
Black Hills (front cover) and the soaring Gateway
Arch in Saint Louis (back cover) attest to the
triumph of great ideas as well as masterful construction. San Francisco's remarkable Golden Gate
Bridge (page 1) and the intricate "Son of Beast"
roller coaster at Paramount's Kings Island in Ohio
(title pages) epitomize engineering virtuosity.

INDEX OF PHOTOGRAPHS